Angels

Millennial Messengers

Seraphim:
n Mitford & Alex Burt, photographers
Justina Hart, author

**For Heidi Burness (born 16 March 1999)
and in memory of Kenneth Arnold (1916-1998)
Carl Ferrarella (1950-1998)
Sarah Francis (1964-1997)
and Brian Charles Mitford (1935-1997)**

First published in 1999
by Seraphim Press
11 Wylde Green Road, Sutton Coldfield, West Midlands B72 1HB

Angels: Millennial Messengers was supported by
the National Lottery through the Arts Council of England

This edition is a limited run of 2000

ISBN 0 9535779 0 2

Set in ITC Kabel book
Printed and bound in Great Britain by W3 Litho, Evesham
Repro by G. Treglown Associates Ltd
Printed on Quatro Silk supplied by Quatro Paper Ltd, Worcestershire

Introduction

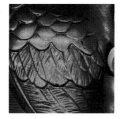  

Any portrayal of angels is an attempt to describe the indescribable. Angels are immaterial, immortal spirits who can be momentarily embodied on earth, but who resist capture on film. They are shape-shifters who dart between heaven and earth at the speed of their own thoughts, their presence perceived in the flickering of lights or stray feathers on the pavement. In archaic traditions they were believed to pass by in a rustle of leaves or in a ripple of water. At times, angels can resemble shining balls of light, at others, tunic-wearing androgynes. They are a hybrid of bird, pagan god, human, and the elements of fire and light.

Angelology is complex because angels are inherently paradoxical. They transcend the logic of our existence, yet have spawned innumerable attempts at rational explanation by some of the greatest minds of all time, including St Augustine, St Thomas Aquinas, Dante and Milton. The impossibility of the angelic body is a challenge which has inspired us to enflesh it in a thousand different forms: since angels can assume new shapes at will and since visionaries provide such diverse accounts, no image or impression can be derided as false. Angels symbolize the ascension of the soul, and thus our yearning for supra-human realms. Pilots glimpse angels hovering in the sky, and NASA astronauts see them floating like monstrous fireflies in the void of space. One Russian cosmonaut reported angels 50 feet tall, flying at 50,000 miles an hour behind his spacecraft.[1]

In recent years, there has been a remarkable upsurge of interest in these heavenly messengers. In a Gallup poll in 1995, 72% of North Americans admitted to believing in the existence of angels; in another, 46% were convinced that they received protection from their own guardian spirit. Around the world, thousands of ordinary people have reported visitations which range from the miraculous to the ridiculous, from evanescent figures at the foot of the bed to sports-car-driving angels. This renewed faith is shared by Christians and New Agers, at opposite ends of the spectrum of belief. Even secularists now claim experience of these mini-gods at key moments in their lives.

What is curious about this trend is the strength of the collective desire to believe. By welcoming belief and discouraging scepticism, the media has fuelled the phenomenon. The word 'angel' appears daily in newspaper headlines, while angelic imagery has been hijacked by advertisers to promote products as diverse as housing and vodka. In a flurry of films including *Wings of Desire* (1987), *A Life Less Ordinary* (1997) and *City of Angels* (1998), angels serve humans as matchmakers, protectors and guides to the afterlife. In 1998, Antony Gormley erected his mammoth sculpture, *Angel of the North*, in Tyneside. Angel sightings remain one of the popular staples of daytime chat shows, while popular culture has spawned hundreds of Internet sites. Extraordinarily, angels are mentioned in around one in every ten pop songs.[2]

It seems bizarre that we should have returned to the supernatural at the end of a secular century. It is hard to ignore angels as millennial omens: lacking reassurance of salvation on earth, we look to the sky for signs. For some, new model angels are more accessible than a distant and old-fashioned deity; their resurgence provides evidence of divine concern. Others covet angels as comforting tokens against an uncertain future and a materialistic present. As creatures of the imagination that we have made flesh (and plastic), they have become our utterly flexible friends. Angels are the magic realists of culture, their historical ambiguity and ineffability enabling us to invest them with whatever meaning we please, however sanitized or sacrilegious. They have been brought down to earth, their mystery crystallized into humanistic beings who can be summoned at will, or artefacts that can be bought and sold. »

[1] 'Angels in space', *Planetary Connection* (Winter 1994/5), p. 11. Additionally, Sophy Burnham writes that three cosmonauts saw "seven giant figures in the form of humans, but with wings and mistlike halos", in *A Book of Angels: Reflections on angels past and present and true stories of how they touch our lives* (New York, Ballantine / Canada, Random House, 1990), pp. 18-19.

[2] Malcolm Godwin. *Angels: An endangered species* (London, Boxtree, 1993), p. 6. Godwin asserts that over the past thirty years, one in every ten pop songs has mentioned an angel.

Against this surprising shift stand ancient esoteric and scriptural traditions that have been obscured by our passion for dumbing down. In our Judaeo-Christian culture, the term 'angel' signifies their function as divine messengers, but winged figures have existed within the human consciousness for four thousand years. Precursors were the winged griffins of Mesopotamia, paintings of the Egyptian goddess Isis; and the Greek gods, Hermes, Eros and Nike. According to tradition, God created a fixed number of angels sometime before the physical universe: fourteenth-century cabbalists managed to calculate an exact figure of 301,655,722. Their role is most clearly defined in the monotheistic religions of Zoroastrianism, Judaism, Christianity and Islam, which stress the distance between man and a single, omnipotent God and thus have the greatest need for spiritual intermediaries.

Although angels pre-eminently serve God, it is mankind which requires them. Without our presence the sublime angels are no more than reflections of themselves. In the *Duino Elegies*, Rilke writes, "you are mirrors: you pour out your beauty / but your faces gather it back to yourselves." The fluctuating popularity and changing face of the celestial realm also provides a fascinating mirror in which we can see and study our own history.

In *East of Eden*, John Steinbeck says: "It would be absurd if we did not understand both angels and devils, since we invented them." *Angels: Millennial messengers* attempts to understand why we have re-invented angels, and why they adopt their particular guise in different cultures. It is difficult to consider angels without expressing some form of belief, at least in their existence as necessary images. It is even harder to confront them with logic. *Seraphim* have endeavoured to tread a path between the two, inspired by the mythical creativity of angels. According to a Talmudic tradition, new angels are formed with every word God speaks, while sixteenth-century Jewish mystics believed that when cabbalists read the Torah, the words, letters and the interpretations of gaps between words all produced angels.[3] Thus man generates angels through images and words, and the angel generates itself out of invisibility. *Seraphim* have photographed their own imaginary angels, as well as more concrete angelic forms that exist as part of our present cultural reality.

Photography has long been used to conjure the surreal and supernatural. Concerned with light, shadow and transitory moments of time, it mimics the elusiveness of the disembodied spirit. It also echoes the angels' paradoxical nature: photographs imply veracity and are used as scientific evidence, but the medium's association with trick pictures and UFO hoaxes; and the possibility of electronic manipulation link it to forgery. The uncertain authenticity of the photograph encapsulates the perceptual ambiguity of angelic encounters which, particularly today, are shrouded in indeterminate reality and religious significance. To see is not necessarily to believe, but to believe might be to see.

Expressed as a journey through the symbolic states of **Light**, **Flesh** and **Stone**, this survey seeks to balance sacred and secular aspects of the present trend. In **Light**, a visual language of radiance and ethereality is adopted to suggest the yearning for angels. **Flesh** documents human imitation of angels, and their commercial incarnation, alongside imaginative recreations of 'real' encounters and modern interpretations of angels' traditional role and purpose.

Both the gravitas and metaphysical lightness of angels must be restored to our collective vision if we are one day to resurrect angels as powerful images of something 'other' than ourselves. The last section is a metaphor for the way in which angels have been pulled to earth within contemporary culture. **Stone** considers ambiguities overshadowed by our desire for beneficent angels, a process that began with their Renaissance humanization. It explores the Angel of Death, Satan, the fallen angels and finally, angels as symbols of resurrection.

[3] Harold Bloom. *Omens of Millennium: The gnosis of angels, dreams, and resurrection* (London, Fourth Estate, 1997), pp. 88-9.

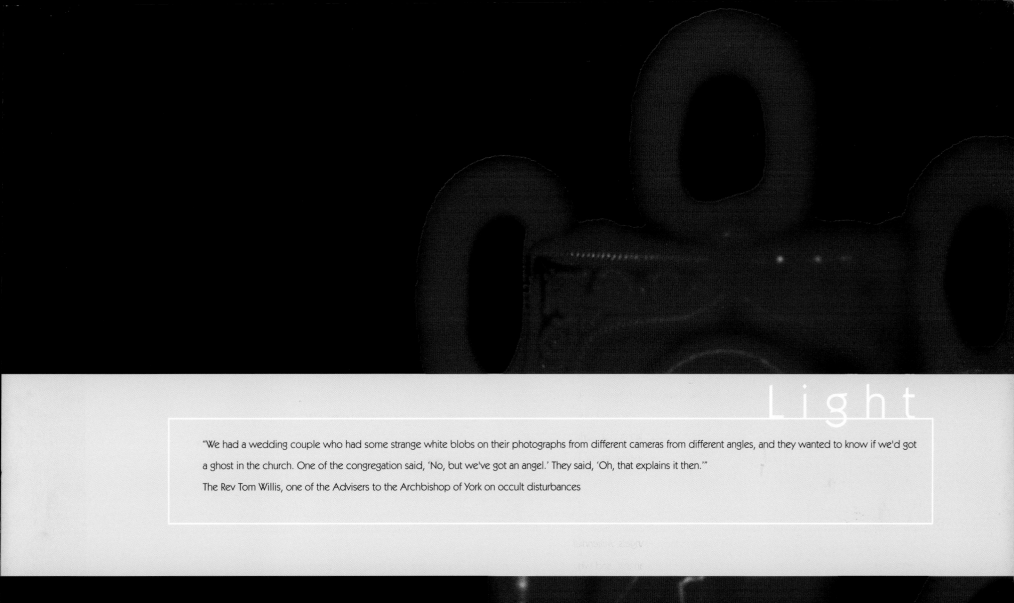

Light

"We had a wedding couple who had some strange white blobs on their photographs from different cameras from different angles, and they wanted to know if we'd got a ghost in the church. One of the congregation said, 'No, but we've got an angel.' They said, 'Oh, that explains it then.'"

The Rev Tom Willis, one of the Advisers to the Archbishop of York on occult disturbances

Modern Messengers

Angels have appeared to some of the greatest prophets, theologians, mystics and visionary poets who ever lived. St Francis and St Teresa of Avila, as well as gnostic, Sufi and cabbalistic seers, saw or heard angels. Djibril (Gabriel) appeared to Muhammad, on what is known as the Night of Power and Glory, to reveal the Koran. Angels have inspired the extraordinary and diverse visions of Dante, Milton, Swedenborg, Blake, and even secular twentieth-century poets such as Rilke and Wallace Stevens. Yet at no other time in history have ordinary people encountered winged beings on the scale on which they are being reported today.

The main characteristics of these contemporary angel encounters are a bright, numinous light accompanied by feelings of warmth, love and peace. According to accounts, messenger spirits can appear in an incredible range of shapes and sizes. Renaissance or Pre-Raphaelite figurative angels with flowing robes and statuesque wings, and angels disguised as humans, are the most frequently observed. Angels also reportedly appear as balls or bars of bright light, invisible heavenly choirs, a scent of flowers or simply as a force, presence or disembodied smile. They descend at times of personal crisis to individuals who claim they gain a sense of protection, inner calm and renewed purpose from the visit.

Many angels seem to bring simple messages, giving counsel to those in distress, strengthening the resolve of the terminally ill, and hovering around altars before individuals kneeling in prayer. Such accounts are comparable to biblical stories in which angels guide, reassure and encourage individuals. Other contemporary angelic activities are more dramatic. Some people attribute their escape from say, a plane or car crash, to miraculous angelic intervention. Angel encounter books recount incredible stories, such as children trapped in a refrigerated meat truck having been freed by dazzling angels.[1] Heavenly helpers dressed as hitchhikers have apparently hauled cars out of mud, while angelic surfers have rescued drowning swimmers. Again, ancient stories can be found to parallel these accounts. Daniel was saved by an angel from the lions' den (Daniel 6:20-2). King Nebuchadnezzar of Babylon saw an angel walking in a furnace into which three Jewish officials had been thrown for refusing to worship a golden image (Daniel 3).

Biblical angels also performed practical deeds, such as releasing St Peter from prison (Acts 12:7-11). But while these spirits were active in God's divine plan, their modern counterparts, not least in those reports stemming from North America, sometimes seem reduced to resolving domestic dilemmas. Latter-day angels have been sighted carrying unwieldy shopping bags, completing tax forms and even helping people to lose weight. Another difference between traditional and modern angels is that biblical angels abruptly disappeared upon completing their tasks, thus de-emphasizing the importance of the angel and directing glory to God. Today, celestial visitors engage with their beneficiaries on a more personal level. Whereas Daniel fell unconscious at the sight of an angel (Daniel 8:15-17), contemporary beholders are often less over-awed. »

"Since the day we were born we have had two Guardian Angels by our side to help and protect us 24 hours a day, 7 days a week. We can call on our Angels to help us anytime of the day or night."

The Official Guardian Angels Home Page

---

[1] John Ronner. *The Angels of Cokeville: And other true stories of heavenly intervention* (Murfreesboro, Tennessee, Mamre Press, 1995), pp. 67-70.

We tend to see angels in human guise because we can identify with them in our secular age. At one end of the encounter spectrum, however, these angels have become superficial and over-abundant, directing us back to ourselves rather than to God. Furthermore, St Paul counsels us: "Be not forgetful to entertain strangers: for thereby some have entertained angels unawares" (Hebrews 13:2). In North America, so many people now live in expectation of experiencing angels, that they are more likely to be mobbed on arrival than to pass unrecognized.

Angels once appeared as mystical messenger figures who provided spiritual solace, inspired grandiose visions and served to subjugate the ego to the will of God. Today, many encounters involve good-looking men and women dressed in virginal white who perform acts of domestic kindness. Since they are easily accessed and tend to convey highly personal, even trivial messages, such angels have been stripped of divine purpose and reinvented as humanitarian agents. The angel who looks like us, but is somehow ennobled, serves less to glorify God than to reassure believers of their own validity and perfectibility. In the extreme, modern angels restore the capacity of believers to have faith in themselves, and act as a superstitious safeguard against the void.

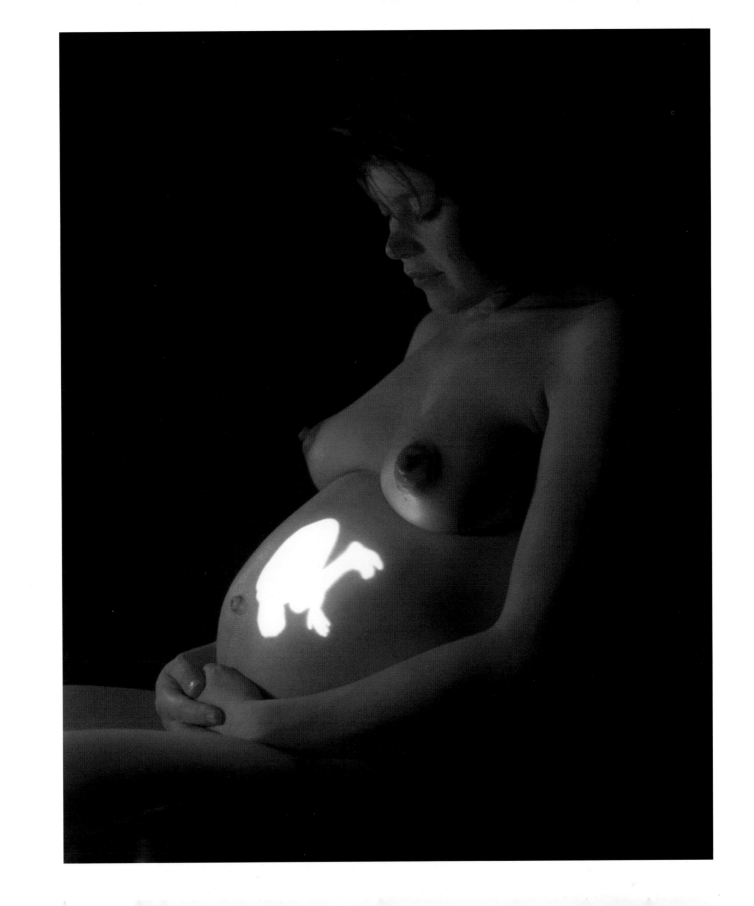

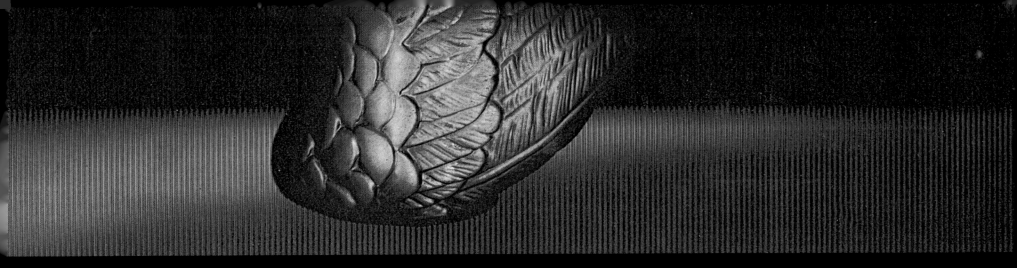

Recording the Invisible

St Thomas Aquinas believed that angels were invisible but could assume bodies when they appeared on earth. Photography is able to re-create this real or imagined moment when the angel is transformed from invisible to embodied being to convey a message: in the dark-room, the blank sheet of paper magically reveals its figures and shapes. A similar transformation occurred when the Archangel Gabriel announced to the Virgin that she was to become the mother of Christ: out of emptiness, the Word was made flesh.

Paradoxically, some forms of photography use the medium's association with visual truthfulness to reinforce 'proof' by means of optical trickery. While the camera was once believed never to lie, it is now accepted that the long exposures and photographic accidents (double exposures, the fogging of film or paper) of the first practitioners, enabled it to convey dream-like states and depict non-existent scenes and apparitions. Creative mistakes were absorbed into photography's visual language and enthusiastically exploited. Uniquely placed to record and represent invisible realms, photography became the natural successor to Victorian supernatural drawings and other visual fantasies.

In 1861, the first reported photograph of a ghost appeared. Probably a double exposure, it launched a spate of images of supernatural phenomena, which did not abate until the First World War. Since the development of photography was founded in the nineteenth-century desire to document and analyse empirical reality, ghostly impressions in faked photographs were used to reassure spiritualists and theosophists that ghosts existed: spiritualists thought that after death a physical being, an astral body remained, which could be summoned through the seance. But other hoax photographs, like the five Cottingley Fairy pictures taken between 1917 and 1920 by Francis Griffiths and Elsie Wright, said more about the desire to believe in a mysterious, unscientific world than about the existence of miniature people with butterfly wings dancing behind the potting shed.

As paranormal beliefs shifted, staged nineteenth-century ghost pictures gave way to ethereal and ectoplasmic images. Photographers like Louis Darget dispensed with optical exposure, which requires a system of lenses, and experimented with direct mental or spiritual projection onto unexposed film. By discarding the camera, these images transcended the hoax status of the photograph and offered »

"In a mind-boggling encounter that may solve one of life's great mysteries, an airline pilot has snapped an unmistakable photograph of an angel!"

North American tabloid, *Weekly World News*, Spring 1998

an alternative form of reality.[1] Similar techniques were used from the 1890s to the 1920s by Darget and others to record mysterious human emanations like 'nervous fluid'. It has been suggested that since these images do not depend on cameras or light, they are more akin to religious relics like the Turin Shroud, believed to be imprinted with the image of Christ.[2]

The discovery that X-rays could be photographed at the end of the nineteenth century led to contemporary experiments with tomography (used to obtain X-ray photographs of parts of the human body), aura and Kirlian photography. In Kirlian imaging (popularized in the 1940s and 1950s), a sheet of film or paper is exposed by placing an object in contact with an electrostatic field. When human hands, a leaf or slice of bread are placed in the stream of charged particles, the object is excited and a corona discharge takes place. The images contain patterns of filamentary blotches and rays which practitioners claim are photographs of the invisible and unique life-force or aura of the object.

While scientists remain sceptical that the Kirlian machine makes anything other than curious pictures, photography itself is capable of conjuring dreams and visions. Angelic encounters, like other mystical and religious experiences, seem so far beyond the bounds of ordinary experience that no matter how reliable witnesses appear, reports inevitably become clichéd and marred by apology and ellipsis. Photography is capable of giving form to the ineffable. The moment of photographic revelation becomes a metaphor for brief but transcendent visionary experience.

The cinema, by contrast, creates the supernatural by using special effects. It has been fascinated by the role of angelic figures since the playful dream sequence in *The Kid* (Charles Chaplin, 1921), in which Chaplin, the foundling child and a little dog; each wearing white shifts and wings; fly, somewhat ineptly, along the street. However, it spools out fantasies that feel real for only as long as the viewer remains in its darkened arena. But on the flat surface of the photograph, images which might have existed in the mind's eye can be resurrected and imbued with an air of authenticity.

Today's spirit photographs might be more commonly expected to convey a sense of mystery, memory or loss than to suggest belief in invisible realms. However, the recent upsurge of interest in the supernatural, coupled with the development of films that can capture regions of the electromagnetic spectrum beyond the reach of the human eye, mean that it may not be long before strange white smudges are proved to be ghosts, or even angels, on film.[3]

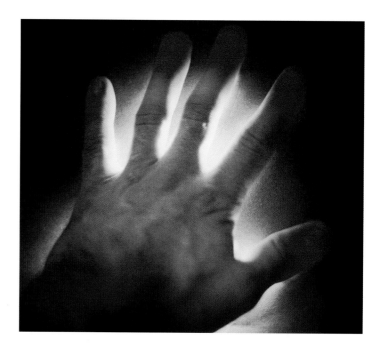

[1] James Roberts. *Frieze*, 40 (May 1998), p. 60. [2] Ibid., p. 61. [3] Andy Coghlan. 'Midnight watch', *New Scientist*, 2165/6/7 (19-26 December 1998 - 2 January 1999), pp. 42-4.

"I felt myself surrounded by a smile. I did not see any being."

"It wasn't something I was seeing with my eyes, but I was seeing it (if you can understand that!)"

Two witnesses describing their angelic encounters

Independence

Initially it seems strange that interest in angels should be renewed on a scale unprecedented since the Middle Ages at a time when church attendance is in sharp decline.[1] Within Christianity, however, there has always been a tension between God and the elevation of spiritual intermediaries to a status that seems to rival His authority.[2] Angels have an in-built tendency to take wing within the popular imagination and soar beyond their station as humble agents of the divine.

In the first century AD, grass roots interest in angels threatened to overwhelm the adoration of Christ, the super-mediator between God and man. To quash this threat, the church insisted that angelic beings did not demand veneration in their own right, but directed humans entirely to God. A new emphasis in teaching meant that where once it had been possible to rank Christ among the angels (also known confusingly as 'sons of God'), He was now distinguished as fully divine. Angels, represented as in the service of Christ, were, on the other hand, created beings, and hence only semi-divine. However, in AD 787, four hundred years after angel worship had been declared idolatrous, a new upsurge in popularity necessitated a stronger ideological stance. The church was forced to establish a limited and carefully defined cult of the archangels, and to legalize the depiction of angels in sculpture and painting.

Angels once again flew out of control between the eleventh and thirteenth centuries when thousands of new names appeared. Although not respected in the Christian calendar, many of these paper angels assumed roles equivalent to minor pagan deities, and were eventually accepted as valid. They could be easily invented by adding the suffix 'el' to names of pagan divinities, or by juggling letters of the Hebrew alphabet.[3] Curiously, some contemporary angel enthusiasts are engaged in a similar practice of fabricating their own private host of spiritual attendants.

St Paul once issued a stark warning against the "worshipping of angels" which some enter into blindly, "vainly puffed up by [their] fleshly mind," (Colossians 2:18). In spite of burgeoning and sometimes misdirected interest in angels, the church has not issued any comparable statement against contemporary angelolatry. Given that some interest in angels manifests at least a nostalgia for traditional structures of belief, it is not inconceivable that the church is quietly complicit. The Church of England remains diffident, but the Catholic *Catechism* published in 1992 reconfirmed that "the existence of angels is a truth of the faith". Meanwhile, clerics in North America are aware that they can swell their congregations simply by preaching a sermon on angels.[4]

Today, some evangelical groups interpret the huge upsurge in angelic encounters as evidence of increased divine concern in a secular world. However, since these spiritual intercessions seem to be more actively pro-human than at any other time in the past two thousand years, this might more accurately reflect a spiritual crisis: the displacement of the need for a compassionate God onto His more user-friendly messenger spirits. Meanwhile, for New Agers searching for spiritual inclusiveness and harmony, angels have escaped traditional religious confines altogether. They are worshipped as free spirits, floating in a pagan universe.

Angels are paradoxical creatures. Ultimately, they cannot be disassociated from the notion of a creator God: without someone to send them, and without a message to deliver, of what use are heaven's errand boys?[5] At the same time, the popularity of angels, which has flared up at historical moments, might be indicative of our metaphysical difficulty in relating to a single, omnipotent divinity. There is the possibility that we have now, as in the Middle Ages, returned angels to the status of gods, and let polytheism in through the back door.

[1] According to a survey by the Office for National Statistics, in 1996 53% of British people said that they "never or practically never" attended religious services, compared with 48% in 1989.

[2] Bloom. *Omens of Millennium*, p. 75.   [3] Gustav Davidson. *A Dictionary of Angels: Including the fallen angels* (New York, The Free Press / London, Collier-Macmillan, 1967), p. 21.

[4] George Howe Colt. 'In search of angels', *Life* (December 1995).   [5] Bloom. Op. cit., p. 71.

The angel is a cultural archetype, or symbol, which has existed for thousands of years. Aristotle believed in "intelligences" and Plato thought that gods and the souls of men were winged, moving "with a lightly rushing motion" between heaven and earth. The angel archetype is the messenger of the higher self, the wise being, the shaman, saint or superhero. In the twentieth century it has been translated into the guardian angels, Superman and Batman, who swapped wings for cloaks, and replaced the dragon-slaying Archangel Michael in the popular imagination.[1]

There is no doubt that there is a strong correlation between sightings of angels and millennial expectancy, just as in the 1950s, the psychologist C. G. Jung believed that the Cold War and the population explosion provided a psychological motivation for projection of unconscious contents onto UFOs. Fanned by evangelical and millenarian movements preaching Armageddon, our collective anxiety has given rise to visionary rumours (global visual stories) of UFOs alongside flocks of compassionate angels. It is in keeping with this theory that angel sightings have been most acute in North America, the home of end-time theology. Reports of encounters have now been corroborated by testimonies from around the world. Angels are also promulgated by the same media that promoted UFOs in the 1950s: there is a tendency to believe and to want angels to be real. The North American tabloid, *Weekly World News*, reported in December 1998 that over 2,800 people claimed to have seen "mysterious winged humanoids" at sacred sites in Jerusalem during the preceding three months. The suggestion was, of course, that they heralded the Second Coming of Christ.[2]

Were he still alive, Jung would doubtless have been fascinated by the nature and scale of these contemporary 'events'. In his book, *Flying Saucers: A modern myth of things seen in the sky*, Jung argued that the ends of eras tend to be accompanied by changes in our conceptions of archetypes, which bring about dramatic transformations of the collective psyche.[3] Since apparently weightless spacecraft are not scientifically plausible, they can be explained as psychological »

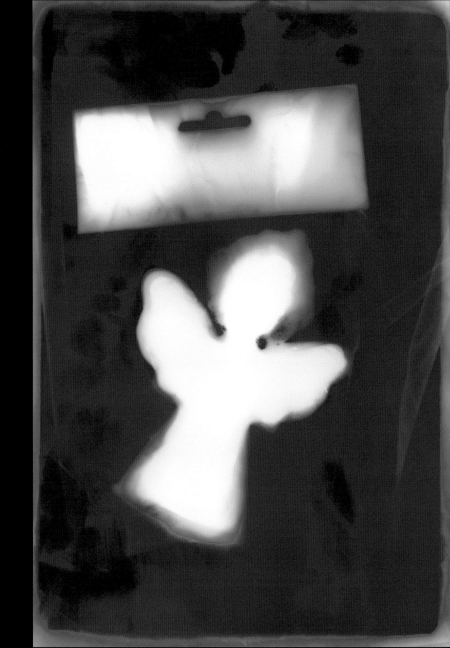

projections of the unconscious, which have a psychic cause. The omnipresence of UFOs in the1950s suggested that projections were motivated by a situation of distress or danger "common to all mankind", which led to collective emotional tension.[4] Jung believed that the UFO's disc-like or spherical shape was an archetypal image that could restore psychic order and unity because it symbolized the totality of the self.

Jung thought belief in heavenly intervention unlikely in a society which had lost the capacity to respond directly to the numinous world: "we cannot get back to that limited world view which in former times left room for metaphysical intervention. Nor can we resuscitate... the Christian hope for an imminent end of the world".[5] Yet this is precisely the hope that has been resurrected today. The visionary rumour of the UFO is in accordance with a scientific age which adopts a technological fable in order to appear rational. However, since angels are a supernatural myth, the angel phenomenon seems to constitute a throwback to a less enlightened age, when every blade of grass was thought to have its own heavenly protector.

Jungian psychology provides a highly plausible explanation for this apparent cultural regression. Faced with the ultimate threat of Apocalypse, we have become fearful of our corruption and unspirituality, and, not seeing help on earth, have turned to ancient, stabilizing figures from the heavens. Only overwhelming symbols of 'otherness' can challenge us to respond to the enormity of the perceived threat. In other words, if what threatens the collective psyche is fear of Apocalyse and the Last Judgement as prophesied in Revelation, then only biblically derived images are potent enough to restore psychic order. By unconsciously projecting onto angels, who certain Christians believe have been sent by God to save the planet, some among us have bypassed the modern urge for rational explanation and resorted to blind faith. Those who do not express conscious credulity can also conjure angels, since, as Jung explains, the rational mind forces the unconscious to resort to particularly vivid projections to make its contents perceived.[6]

Yet if our quest is for God's army, why have we recruited hosts of remarkably benign and beneficent angels to act as our saviours? During the course of the past five hundred years we have softened and rationalized angels into symbols of human perfectibility, rather than images of the divine. Being only indirectly in touch with the numinous world, we tend not to see the terrifying angel in all its glory, but a less potent and psychically dangerous image: St Bridget (?1303-73) believed that such a vision would cause a mortal to die of love. The pre-eminence of the profoundly human and humanitarian angelic image is entirely in keeping with the spirit of our age.

Until the advent of the year 2001, it seems likely that the more religiously-minded will continue to perceive angels, while others will project the hope for salvation onto shiny discs in the sky.

Everybody's Birthday Book   George and Cornelia Kay

THE FRIENDSHIP BOOK   1988

THE FEMALE APPROACH   Ronald Searle   MACDONALD

* * HAPPENINGS * * *   821

I AM WITH YOU ALWAYS   JARROLD

A Book of Comfort   Elizabeth Goudge

LOOK BACK IN LOVE   By Adrian Bury, R.W.S.   CS

LIFE AFTER LIFE   RAYMOND A. MOODY, JR., M.D.

THE CONQUEST OF HAPPINESS   Bertrand Russell   14

LOVE IS A COUPLE   Fr. Chuck Gallagher, S.J.   IMAGE

Nina Epton   Love and the English   2192

Ernest Hemingway   A Farewell to Arms   2

RIVER and GILLESPIE   PL 1555   THE SECRETS OF LIFE   STUART WILDE   WDI

Michael Jose

erenberg
H. Calero

Kovacs Stein and
Ann Schuler   SPHERE

HUTCHINSON

ARIAL   Foulsham

Day
endar   STEIN
is Schutz

Rand
McNally

Collins

MICHAEL
JOSEPH

DDER & STOUGHTON

BUS

Hutchinson

THE DICTIONA
DREA

Collecting Inexpensive Ar

FORTY P.

Daxter   Pure Love

Body Language

Every Other Sunday   Jean R.

THE FANCY DRE   ACE BOOKS

581   BODILY COMA

ENGLAND

Alberto Moravia

Alberto Mora

A DIARY WITHOUT DATES

THE NEW BOOK OF DAYS   MARCUS   WOODWARD

Flesh

"Angels have come near the planet because we need to awaken; we must do the work to help the planet because it's in dire straits. It's in every aspect of my work: singing, dancing, healing. Whatever I'm doing, the angels are there. It's like they're using every channel that isn't bad or wicked that's available. My last dog was an angel dog."

Vicky Copestake

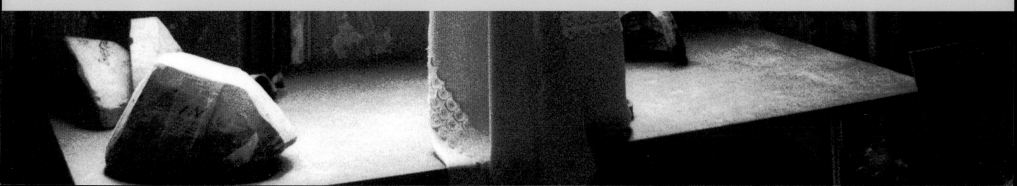

Corporeality

Old Testament writers pictured the earliest biblical angels as human males and so instigated a patriarchal angelology. Abraham washed the feet of three angelic visitors before preparing them a meal of veal, bread and cheese (Genesis 18:1-8). Jacob wrestled so corporeal an angel that his thigh was put out of joint (Genesis 32:25).

Our attempts at representing the bodiless, sexless angels have come full circle. Like their Old Testament predecessors, modern angels tend to look indistinguishable from human males, although the female of the species and black angels are occasionally allowed to enter our heavenly ranks. Brad Silberling's sexy, designer angels in *City of Angels* (1998) are so bereft of traditional Christian iconography – wings, and a halo of bright light – that only the flapping of the actors' long black coats in the wind is redolent of flight or supernatural lightness. The ancestors of these earthly angels were actually the humanized angels of the Italian Renaissance, rather than crude attempts at embodiment by biblical scribes.

Christian artists depicted angels as wingless, toga-wearing males until the fourth century AD, when the growing emphasis on spirituality within the early church necessitated a new image. Grappling with the problem of representing biblical angels – either utterly bizarre as in Ezekiel's vision of beings with four faces, inspired by Assyrian and Egyptian art (Ezekiel 1:5-10); or very human as in Abraham's encounter at Mamre (Genesis 18:2) – artists turned to Greek victories and figures of Hermes for inspiration. Borrowing ultimately from birds, with their sacred connotations, angels were transformed into beautiful, winged young men. They often appeared with partial bodies or as disconnected, winged heads until the late Gothic stress on their ideal beauty led to the angels' extreme etherealization. In German artist Matthias Grünewald's *Isenheim Altarpiece*, angels are given only fragile embodiment and painted as diffuse circles of light. Giotto's fourteenth-century angels were invested with golden haloes, naturalistic faces and upper bodies: in *The Mourning of Christ* (1302-6), the angels' acrobatic anguish reflects the expressions of the static human mourners. Their lower bodies, which dissolve into the sky, suggest the speed of their flight.

As faith in the supernatural workings of the universe gave way to a reliance on scientific investigation of natural laws, Renaissance painters gradually drew the angels down to the ground. Paradoxically, as they became more insubstantial in the eyes of theologians, new humanistic beliefs rendered them more naturalistic on canvases and church walls. In Fra Angelico's *The Annunciation* (1432), his genuflecting angel is invested with rainbow plumage, human form and robes, yet still appears androgynous and insubstantial. Twenty years later, Piero della Francesca brought the Archangel Gabriel literally to his knees in *The Annunciation*, (*The Polyptych of St Anthony*). Here, Gabriel appears to be made firmly of flesh, as though gravity has anchored his spirit.[1] »

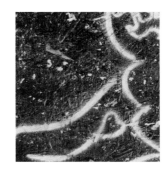 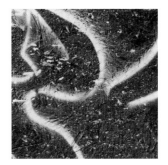 

[1] Godwin. *Angels*, p. 162.

"He was dressed in armour like that of a Roman centurion and his presence seemed to fill the room. I was in awe of him and felt he must have had to leave some vast spiritual battle just to keep me company."

A woman describing her angelic encounter

By the sixteenth century, the angelic norm had shifted from small, floating figures with two-dimensional wings, to life-size flesh and blood beings with realistic, bird-like wings. Leonardo da Vinci and Caravaggio studied the flight mechanics of swans, geese and eagles to devise the muscular wing structures required to keep these heavier angels airborne. Michelangelo drew humans and angels even more tightly together. In his *Last Judgement* in the Sistine Chapel, he divested his angels entirely of wings. But the Catholic Church couldn't come to terms with his finishing touch, male genitalia, and had the offending, unangelic flesh painted over.[2]

While these glorious angels are clearly nonsensical – one contemporary angelologist has speculated that an angel weighing 90 kilograms would need a wingspan of between 12 and 40 metres to get off the ground[3] – the baroque vision continues to epitomize our idea of angels. After the seventeenth century, artists slowly lost interest in angels, employing chubby cherubs – which had been omnipresent in baroque art – as church space-fillers. The transformation of the cherubim from their origins as Assyrian winged beasts with human faces, to the sword-wielding angels of Genesis who bar the way back to paradise, and finally into the playful male infants of Rubens, illustrates how the angels have been softened and sentimentalized over the centuries.

Angels are now more commonly portrayed in films than in paintings. In 1946, Frank Capra created his famous and elderly angel, Clarence Oddbody, whose whimsicality stresses his status as purely imaginary product. In *It's a Wonderful Life,* Clarence, an "Angel Second Class", saves local hero George Bailey from committing suicide, thus earning his wings: "every time a bell rings, an angel gets his wings." But by the time of *Michael* (1996), the great Archangel has become a paunchy, womanizing, cigarette-smoking sinner. Adding a pair of glorious white wings to Archangel Michael – John Travolta in boxer shorts – seems more like an offensive afterthought than a joke.

Since there is no longer any discernible difference between angels and humans, we are left with humans pretending to be angels, and rather tarnished post-Enlightenment angels at that. We must look to celebrities who are queuing up to strap on golden wings and plastic haloes, to embody our very grounded ideals.

[2] Ibid., p. 158.   [3] Ibid., p. 168.

Attributes

Angels are traditionally believed to be invisible or to possess ethereal bodies, which makes the phrase 'heavenly body' a contradiction in terms. Yet, for centuries, angels have been portrayed as physically and mentally perfect human beings. Angels were envisaged as beings who exemplified human characteristics in their purest forms, and we have striven to mimic their imagined perfection. Since we have always been considered less perfect than angels, the angelic ideal is symbolic of aspiration rather than attainability. »

Since the sixteenth century, the adjective 'angelic' has been used to describe a person who resembles an angel in attributes or actions. Angelic virtues are essentially Christian and traditionally include purity, selflessness, wisdom, good judgement and innocence. Children, whose guardian angels are believed to occupy a special place in heaven, have had a long association with the angelic; they are sometimes termed 'little angels'. The link between feminine beauty and angels was popularized by Victorian paintings of female guardian angels who were depicted protecting children and young lovers. Today, nurses are often described as angels, and people suffering from Aids sometimes imagine themselves free from disease, transfigured into angels. The British woman, Sally Becker, who rescued 170 people from Bosnia in 1993-4, was dubbed the 'Angel of Mostar' by the press. Princess Diana has been elevated to iconic status and compared to an angel since her death. She is to appear with wings and a halo in an animation called *Princess Diana Saves the World*.

Victorian husbands idealized their wives as domestic angels, as in Coventry Patmore's poem, 'The Angel in the House'. The perfect Victorian woman was not only ultra-feminine – sensitive, frail and sweet-tempered – but also meek and dutiful, as this passage from Wilkie Collins' *The Woman in White* (1859-60) shows: "I am dark and ugly, and she is fair and pretty. Everybody thinks me crabbed and odd... and everybody thinks her sweet-tempered and charming... In short, she is an angel; and I am –". Pre-Raphaelites like Edward Burne-Jones, who utilized pagan as well as medieval Christian imagery, eroticized their female angels. Building on this tradition, Josef von Sternberg transformed Marlene Dietrich into the erotic angel, Lola, in *The Blue Angel* in 1930. In today's tabloids nubile young women are frequently referred to as angels and the word is incorporated into the names of beauty salons and strip clubs.

As angels have been debased as religious symbols, so they have been brought closer to earth and differences between the species of humans and angels blurred. Humans are considered to have a greater capacity for perfection, and angels to be more sensual and corporeal. The appeal of the blue angel becomes the appeal of that impossible fantasy, the virginal whore, or of the angel on the verge of a fall. »

"How do you get the body of an ANGEL? A. Cheat B. Get a dog C. Smoke heavily"

Advert for *Women's Health* magazine, December 1998

Similarly, where we once considered talent God-given, to describe human ability as 'angelic' now exalts the intelligence of the human being, rather than the inherent perfection of the angel. Stripping angels of their difference has enabled them to be softened into a ubiquitous advertising motif. Cutely sexy angelic imagery is used to sell clothes, alcohol and face cream. Wings and haloes stress the supposedly unparalleled quality of the product and the moral virtuosity of the purchaser, while the fluttering angel happily reinforces the capitalist dream that perfection can be bought.

"I've got this really neat receipt that says, 'One large Shearer shirt, £999'."

Kevin Waugh, who catapulted a giant replica of Alan Shearer's Newcastle United shirt over Antony Gormley's sculpture, Angel of the North

Angels and Endorphins

Sixteenth-century science was responsible for pushing angels out of the sky. Once Copernicus had proved that the earth was not the centre of the universe, it was difficult to believe that angels moved the planets around or tilted the axis of the world. Belief in the concrete reality of heaven and hell was eroded and angels turned into a metaphor, a way of approaching a receding and unknowable deity. Now that God no longer lived above the fixed stars in the *coelum empyraeum* (the highest heaven), the famous Renaissance debates about the number of angels that could fit on the head of a pin and the precise structure of the angelic hierarchy, were not so much intellectual whimsy as serious investigations into the nature of reality. Angelologists had effectively become early cosmological physicists.

In our materialistic age, in which man has been reduced to a collection of molecules and God is either very far distant or interpreted as a Jungian symbol of wholeness, disembodied intelligences have still managed to flutter through holes in the modern fabric of non-belief. The Pre-Raphaelite artist, Edward Burne-Jones, was quoted as saying: "the more materialistic science becomes, the more angels shall I paint: their wings are my protest in favour of the immortality of the soul." [1] One explanation for the present revival of angelicism, which shows us grasping at the fall-out of faith, is our further disenchantment with scientific reductionism. At the same time, science is being used to provide compelling explanations for the perceived reality of supernatural phenomena. »

"I began to pray and needed a knight in shining armour to rescue me. Moments later, an amazing black sports car pulled up. The dark-tinted window rolled down and a blonde man leaned out and shouted: 'Oi! You! Leave her alone!' The man who'd been harassing me stumbled into the road, whereupon the angel drove off."

A woman describing her angelic encounter

[1] From a lecture by Oscar Wilde called 'The English Renaissance of Art', given on 9 January 1882 in New York and published in his *Essays and Lectures*. Stephen Wildman and John Christian. *Edward Burne-Jones: Victorian artist-dreamer* (New York, The Metropolitan Museum of Art, 1990), pp. 237-8.

There are fundamental sociological and psychological explanations for why people see what they see. Writers of angel encounter books are fond of asserting that witnesses are in no doubt that they have seen strictly angelic apparitions. Written accounts do not corroborate this neat assumption, however. Witnesses commonly stress that experiences "might have been" angelic, or state that they later chose angelic intervention as the most helpful explanation. What you perceive is, of course, dependent on cultural background and on what you expect to see. It is hardly surprising that more religious than non-religious people report encounters. If Jesus is perceived as black in Ethiopia, but white in the West, it also follows that the majority of celestial visitors reported in Britain and North America conform to pre-conceived notions that angels are asexual, wear white robes, and have blonde hair and blue eyes.

By implying that consciousness plays a key role in the so-called physical universe, quantum physics is being used to offer a radical, scientific foundation for cultural differences in the interpretation of phenomena. The new physics aims to discover that there is no such thing as Newton's single, observable physical world, but instead a number of possible, co-existing realities. The human brain intuitively edits out all those realities it cannot accept and perceives the one arbitrary reality that it wants to see. Perception is thus understood as a democratic form of learned behaviour which results in people from the same culture constructing the same reality.

New physicists would argue that the thousands of people who believed they saw the statue of the Virgin Mary move in the Republic of Ireland in the mid 1980s were experiencing a mass hallucination. Social or political stress caused witnesses to create a collective, phantasmagoric reality: they actually did see the statue move. Journalists in Ireland confirmed that people were very depressed about the spiritual health of the nation at that time.[2] Similar explanations could be given for the mass vision of angels at the Battle of Mons on 23 August 1914, or for the 70,000 people in Fátima, Portugal, who saw a dancing sun and the smiling face of the Virgin on 13 October 1917.[3] The population of America's 'Bible belt', where 93% believe in angels,[4] may therefore be experiencing a collective hallucination in which angelic apparitions have been created as the perceived reality, perhaps in response to a deep spiritual malaise.

Neurological explanations are also being proposed by some neurophysiologists and paranormal researchers to explain why certain individuals perceive supernatural phenomena. A popular theory is that apparitions can appear as a result of mini-seizures in a part of the brain called the temporal lobe, believed to have a strong connection with mystical and religious experience. Extremes of hunger and exhaustion, as well as electromagnetic changes in the environment, have been shown to produce vivid hallucinations comparable to UFO encounters in otherwise normal individuals. When the body is in pain or shock it also releases endorphins which bring about feelings of blissfulness and even »

[2] Colm Tóibín (ed.). *Seeing is Believing: Moving statues in Ireland* (Laois, Ireland, Pilgrim Press, 1985), p. 17.   [3] Michael Talbot. *Mysticism and the New Physics* (London, Routledge & Kegan Paul, 1987), pp. 125-6.   [4] *Front Row* (BBC Radio 4, 1 May 1998).

hallucinations. It is thought that at such times, comforting images may be seized upon by the individual's unconscious to enable them to respond to the crisis. Such mental and physical changes in the beholder could explain the type of angelic encounter that occurs in life-threatening situations.

It has been known for many years that schizophrenic patients sometimes describe visions of demons or angels. Psychologists and psychiatrists have also linked belief in magic with certain mental and developmental abnormalities, and suggest that sufferers are more likely to see paranormal phenomena. Psychedelic substances have similarly been proven to induce incredible apocalyptic visions. The archaic use of hallucinogenic substances such as peyote and fly-agaric

mushrooms for magic and ritual purposes is well documented. Basque director Julio Medem explored such perceptual ambiguities in his 1997 film, *Tierra*. His protagonist, Angel, who is presumed to have fallen to earth, relates the film's other-worldly voice-over. However, the audience remains unsure whether Angel is a visionary who hears angelic voices, or suffers from a split personality and an over-active imagination.

It is possible that scientific evidence might one day be found to tip angels off their pinhead and enable them to be taken seriously again as real entities. However, such theories do not negate the validity of the supernatural visions themselves, nor damage the angel as an ancient and abiding image.

"Even people who are entirely compos mentis and in full possession of their senses can sometimes see things that do not exist."

C. G. Jung, Flying Saucers

"I will always believe that angels exist. I am convinced I have three helpers who are to hand when I need."
Paul Delves

Encounter Books

Since the early 1990s, so-called angel encounter books have flooded New Age, esoteric and, latterly, mainstream bookshops in North America and Britain. Populist texts such as Joan Wester Anderson's *Where Angels Walk: True stories of heavenly visitors* (1992), which appeared on the *New York Times* best-seller list for over a year, have responded to but also fuelled the angel new wave.

Writers track present-day celestial activity on earth by sifting through letters in response to 'Have you seen an angel?' adverts, and then sub-dividing stories according to categories of encounter. Chapters are typically devoted to children's experiences, angelic road rescues, angels at bedsides and deathbeds, angelic experiences in wartime, and everyday encounters. This approach gives the bizarre impression that angels are trained professionals who operate as heavenly policemen, doctors and nursemaids. It is redolent of medieval angelology, when it was believed that every named angel had its own discrete function.

Encounter book titles usually incorporate the words 'real' or 'true' to add credibility: *Touched by Angels: True cases of close encounters of the celestial kind* (1992) by the North American, Eileen Elias Freeman, and *Angels: True stories of how they touch our lives* (1993) by British nurse and missionary, Hope Price, are examples. Authors argue that since thousands of normal, sane people have seen angels, then they must exist, and do so in line with the writer's often Christian or New Age bias. For example, Price states that for the purpose of her book she chose to ignore all accounts not "in line with the Bible's teaching".[1] Other encounter books espouse the logic that since angels seem to have a positive effect on people's lives – helping them cope with illness, rescuing them from potential disaster – then their main purpose must be helping individual humans, regardless of whether or not those individuals are deserving or believe in God. There is a contradiction between these encounters and the Scriptures, in which angels only exceptionally intervene in the lives of ordinary humans.

In 1431 French heroine, St Joan of Arc, was burnt at the stake on the pretext that her visions of Michael and other angels and saints were "false and diabolical". At a time when only the Inquisition seemed to know whether you had encountered an angel or a devil in disguise, it was foolhardy to report such visions. However, when a culture no longer stigmatizes individuals for expressing belief in the supernatural, they are then free to report long-buried dream encounters, fantasies and visions: interestingly, research suggests it is this public confession of angelic encounters that is the new phenomenon, rather than the sightings themselves.[2] Such is the sense of specialness conferred on angel witnesses in North America by writers and talk show hosts, that those who have experienced angels feel doubly blessed, first by the angel and secondly by societal approval. These flexible, friendly spirits seem to be easily witnessed and lazily assimilated into our pick 'n' mix approach to religion. Consequently, there is a book, and type of angel, to match every stratum of belief.

There is no doubting the sincerity of many of these latter-day accounts of being touched by angels, nor that they make compelling reading. However, in some encounter books the emphatic re-telling of angelic visitations seems organized in such a way as to induce belief through fear, rather than to encourage a more open-minded response. In *A Book of Angels*, Sophy Burnham tells how a young woman, terrified when walking alone at night through a cemetery, was transported over a bridge to safety by an angel after she had spoken the words, "In the name of Christ, save me". However, when the same woman was later raped at knife-point, the angel she expected would save her, failed to materialize. Burnham sentationalizes this story by adding her own glib yet horrifying explanation: "perhaps she was helped at the cemetery from something worse than rape."[3]

Encounter books and their concomitant culture are dangerous because they encourage the vulnerable to seek spirits and succour where there may only be absence: naturally, the more you read the more you feel open to interpreting chance events in your own past as angelic intervention. And since many among us have harboured a childhood desire to grow wings and fly, it involves only a short imaginative leap to put one's own guardian spirit into orbit. Of course, if you do not buy into this superstitious culture, you risk offending the angel at your shoulder and jeopardizing your future safety.

[1] Hope Price. *Angels: True stories of how they touch our lives* (London, Macmillan, 1993), p. 4.

[2] Glennyce S. Eckersley. *An Angel at My Shoulder: True stories of angelic experiences* (London, Rider, 1996), p. 1.   [3] Burnham. *A Book of Angels*, pp. 74-8.

Therapy

North American self-help guides give new-fangled names to celestial cohorts, styling them cheerleaders, worry extinguishers, prosperity brokers and winged weight watchers. Angels are fun-loving, low-budget life coaches, they assert, who can be coaxed into your daily existence through a mishmash of 'angel mail', meditation, channelling, joss sticks, and by wearing flowing white clothes. Keen to share their "antistress, antigravity, and antiaging secrets",[1] angels wait in the wings to tidy your desk, eradicate debts and stop you bingeing on junk food. Like fairy godmothers, they wave magic wands but ask for nothing in return. Their existence is not open to debate.

It is easy to dismiss these seriously lightweight specimens as nursemaids and psychotherapists for the undiscriminating, yet these angels – recreated as invisible best friends – are serving as a major source of comfort for Middle Americans who feel alienated by traditional forms of worship. Angels appeal to ageing baby-boomers who, realizing the American dream has failed to minister to their spiritual needs, crave religiously-affiliated substitutes to guarantee their immortal survival. They appeal to the under-valued, to those lost in the cultural wasteland and murky morality of daytime TV. Uncomfortable dealing with the starkness of sin and repentance, salvation-seekers are drawn to the inchoate, pliable nature of revisionary spirits.

"The really critical attraction of angels", said George Howe Colt writing in *Life* magazine in 1995, "may be their unconditional love. So many angel seekers I meet tell me of hurt, lonely childhoods."[2] The belief that angels minister to the whole spectrum of humanity, is shared by the thousands of elderly Americans who have made the pilgrimage to the Disneyesque Precious Moments Chapel in Missouri, »

[1] Terry Lynn Taylor. *Messengers of Light: The angels' guide to spiritual growth* (Tiburon, California, H J Kramer, 1990), p. xx.

[2] Colt. 'In search of angels', *Life* (December 1995).

one man's non-denominational monument to everyday tragedy and pain. The temple's walls and ceiling are cluttered with painted cartoon angels, each based on an episode from the life of a real child or adolescent who died prematurely, while signs read, "No more tears". Angels pluck average, even unworthy, citizens from obscurity through their ministrations, and pack them off to heaven. As one popular guide puts it, "Their main function is to keep you from feeling unimportant in this vast sea of humanity." [3]

This ethos is promulgated by America's 'angel community', which encompasses collectors' clubs, awareness seminars, healing circles, magazines, talk shows and Internet sites. Collectors' clubs are a forum for angel obsessives to exchange figurines alongside stories about how, for instance, angels saved them from slipping into the Grand Canyon. At angel circles, believers convene to pray for celestial assistance to help ailing relatives or to alleviate loneliness and fear. Services at the First Church of Angels take the form of 'angel power healing circles', metaphysical healing supposedly mediated by angels. But, as Colt points out, believers are not self-satisfied sentimentalists. Many tithe their income, work with Aids patients or march in peace vigils: "What's wrong with believing in them if they make the world a better place?" argues one devotee.[4]

This brand of angelicism barely pretends to have even tenuous connections with traditional forms of revelation or religion. The Koran teaches that it is impossible to invoke angels. In ancient occult lore, supplicants could ask angels to intervene in times of need for peaceful purposes, but also to destroy enemies. However, »

"All you have to do is define the situation and name the angel who is supposed to take charge of it. A custom-designed angel will arrive and take on the job. In this way, you can draw to you your own personal flock of angels."

Terry Lynn Taylor, *Messengers of Light*

[3] Taylor. Op. cit., p. 8. [4] Colt. Op. cit.

nowhere does it indicate that they can be adopted so effortlessly. This is Christianity stripped of content and rigour, which promotes a vision of an all-inclusive heaven to mirror its proponents' sentimental notions of perfectibility. It is akin to asking the tooth fairy or Father Christmas for help.

At the same time, the overwhelming desire for angels reveals the lack of effective societal constructs that should provide protection and security. Believers have formed their own unorthodox, nurturing communities which offer meaning through an all-embracing kind of love. In parts of North America, at least, New Age angels have become the hard-working therapeutic consolers and miracle workers of the hurt, the bereaved and the lonely.

Free Will

The angels, although created more perfectly in the image of God than man, once felt threatened by his existence. God burned to extinction the angels of peace and truth, the hosts beneath them, and a legion of administering angels for objecting to the creation of man. The Koran and the apocryphal Book of Adam and Eve aver that Satan fell because he refused to bow as commanded before Adam, the newly-made creature of clay.

Our relationship to angels is interpreted very differently in various traditions. Some think that we are a parody of the angels, while others believe that our *raison d'être* is to strive to imitate the angels' purely spiritual intellect, and hence, the majesty of God. Angels help Christians to achieve salvation, presiding over the sacraments and carrying prayers heavenward. Equally, according to Muhammad, angels are sent to find humans who seek to know God: thus fulfilling the purpose for which they were made. For the humanist, the highest part of man is angelic: in *Paradise Lost*, Milton's Adam and Eve are highly angelic, and his angels eat, drink and make love like men. The pious and mystical Franciscan monks aimed not to imitate angels but to become them, so that the soul might attain eventual union with God.[1] Still others believe that we were actually created to supplant the angels.

Man of course enjoys free will as well as sensory experience of which the angels are generally believed to be deprived. According to one form of church doctrine, the angels were invested with free will which they had to surrender at the moment they were created. The young angels were offered an irrevocable choice between turning toward God, in which case they became forever fixed in good, or away from God, and becoming rooted in evil.[2] In our present individualistic age, we might abhor the idea of the perfect angelic existence, which is effectively mechanistic. Angels could be compared to forms of artificial intelligence since they are wise like God, yet are created to obey the divine command unerringly. The seraphim, for instance, are so rapt with the beauty of God that they spend their entire lives chanting 'Holy, holy, holy' in praise of their maker.

In other traditions, however, angels retained their freedom. According to the Greek theologian, Origen of Alexandria, all angels were created equal and free, but some chose to drift away from God. Angels who drifted into the dirty lower air became human, while those who fell furthest were metamorphosed into demons. Origen's angels are not spiritual automata since they must have their own rationality which enables them to challenge the will of God.

Milton's suggestion that both angels and man stand or fall by their own strength rather than God's grace, is heretical. God says, "Freely they stood who stood, and fell who fell" (III 102), but this freedom of will only has significance because God wishes obedience as a sign of faithful love. Milton's Satan is conscious that he has used his divinely appointed freedom to damn himself for all eternity. He suffers remorse and despair for his vaulting ambition, before choosing to align himself with evil.

In accordance with Miltonic humanism, in *Wings of Desire* (1987), Wim Wenders re-configures angels and invests them with free will. Writing in *The Logic of Images* in 1986, Wenders says that Damiel and Cassiel were conceived as rebel angels, imprisoned by God in Berlin after the Second World War and demoted to the status of passive observers. Wenders originally intended that Damiel (who perches on the statue, the Angel of Peace), should choose to become mortal not in order to overcome his impassivity, nor ultimately to experience the fullness of a physical life, but in the hope of releasing "prodigious energies" which will bring peace to mankind.[3] The film-maker's extraordinary proposition is that the angels are so humanistic that they are willing to sacrifice omniscient immortality for our salvation.

---

[1] Godwin. *Angels*, p. 239.

[2] Davidson. *A Dictionary of Angels*, p. xvii.

[3] The Angels believe that their 'changing sides' might cause energies to be invested in the archangel who lives in 'the Angel of Peace': "the great hope is that, by releasing this energy, he might become a real 'angel of peace', and help to bring peace to the world." Wim Wenders. *The Logic of Images: Essays and conversations*, tr. M. Hoffmann (London, Faber and Faber, 1992), p. 81.

Angels 'Я' Us

Beyond their obvious associations with Renaissance art, these days many non-churchgoers tend to think of angels as seasonal accessories. Synonymous with Christmas in the same way that eggs are with Easter, they have become the guardians of the tree and carol, unearthed from the attic and secured on their bed of needles in time for *It's a Wonderful Life*.

Every November, hosts of cardboard, plastic and neon angels fill shop windows, are festooned in street light displays, and splashed across magazines next to Christmas gift ideas. Barring the tinsel-winged children in school nativity plays, these kitsch angels are divorced from any deeper association with the Annunciation or the birth of Christ. Their haloes, harps and trumpets are designed simply to engender feelings of goodwill as a prelude to purchase. They do not sing or bear spiritually-inspired tidings of great joy, but enunciate only the message, 'buy!' In Birmingham, where councillors abolished Christmas in 1998 in favour of the politically correct 'Winterval' so as not to offend ethnic minorities, the city retained certain "traditional images" including angels.[1] This appeared not to be because of angelology's rich, multicultural history – angels feature strongly in all the world's major religious traditions, both Eastern and Western – but because they are seen as blandly celebratory. Angels have become the secular ciphers of an annual spending spree.

Peer beyond December, however, and it soon becomes clear that angels are no longer just for Christmas. By investing in wings 'n' things, you can now buy the comforting illusion of year-round protection. Sweat shirts with the bold declaration 'I am an angel', Fiorucci cherub-embossed T-shirts, shiny silver rucksacks crafted in the shape of wings, angel print boxer shorts and pyjamas are all readily available. Angel chocolates, dolls, candelabra, plaques, stationery, table mats, tea towels and even hand-painted toilet seats decorated with floating cherubim are sold all year round.

At present, there are only a handful of shops in Britain dealing exclusively in angel goods. In North America, which boasts an organisation called HALOS (Helping Angel Lovers Own Stores), set up to encourage enthusiasts to become entrepreneurs, angel emporia have taken off. Shops have contrived names such as *A Wing and A Prayer*, *Cheerful Cherub* ('Catholic-style angels and rubber stamps'), *Believe in Angels* ('angel bumper stickers') and *Ark Angels*. There is even a shop devoted solely to 'angel prosperity products'. When asked to explain his phenomenal success, Denny Dahlmann, founder of HALOS and the store, *Angel Treasures*, replied that his customers were "buying good feelings". Consumers believe that angels can "be counted on to help them with their lives", he added.[2] Commercialization has trivialized angels into the "cotton candy of theology".[3] Stores convert plastic, tin, plaster and porcelain decorations into talismans which engender nebulous feelings of enhanced well-being and spirituality.

Collecting paperweight or key-ring angels for your household shrine involves replacing more substantive expressions of belief with lucky charms, which is not dissimilar to buying relics in the hope of securing a place in heaven. It seems ominous that the inherently elusive angels have today been nailed to the wall, or used as doorstops and toilet flushers: being trapped in a domestic cage might make it difficult for the angels to deliver messages to earth from on high when it really matters.

> "Christmas wouldn't be complete without an angel on top – or below – your tree."

Advert for Thierry Mugler perfume range called 'Angel'

[1] Andy Burrows. 'Clerics slam living in a Winterval wonderland', *The Birmingham Post* (9 November 1998).

[2] James R. Lewis and Evelyn Dorothy Oliver. *Angels A to Z* (Detroit, Michigan, Visible Ink Press, 1996), p. 24.

[3] Colt. 'In search of angels', *Life* (December 1995).

Technological Angels

Mythological messengers like Hermes, the Greek god of communication, were given wings emblematic of power, speed and spirit, to enable them to soar into the air; which was once considered sacred and beyond human reach. This old order was shattered in 1903 by Wilbur and Orville Wright's first powered flight. Since then we have hijacked the angelic attribute of flight and, mimicking the birds, climbed higher and faster in aeroplanes and rockets in our attempts to map the universe.

Whereas the stars were once regarded as angels – the angels (including Satan) were sometimes called 'morning stars' – today's angelic messengers are often man-made. Angels can be viewed as an elegant metaphor for our network of modern, message-bearing communications systems: aeroplanes carry mail and men; surveillance systems monitor and protect; satellites are international purveyors of information; and the Internet is a global communications system. Like traditional angels, satellite telecommunication systems transmit messages to earth from the heavens. Today, many people are employed principally in the transmission of messages, sending and receiving a constant stream of information by phone, fax and e-mail. The Internet, itself an angelic system, is the natural home for hundreds of angel sites and chat rooms, which resemble tiny, feelgood shrines.

Just as traditional angels were believed to be invisible but capable of becoming visible, and able to move through space at the speed of their own thoughts,[1] so technological angels transport messages invisibly and instantaneously in the form of digital signals and electromagnetic waves. Angels are small enough for their entire population to be squeezed onto the head of a pin, and as large as Azrael, the Islamic Angel of Death, who is vaster than the heavens. Today, minute microchips form complex networks that interlink to encircle the world, like Djibril (Gabriel) whose arms stretched from the east to the west when he appeared to Muhammad to reveal the Koran. Modern angels, like their older counterparts, can be bad as well as benign: rockets transmit death, aeroplanes can fail and crash, and computers can carry viruses. The names for several of these viruses even incorporate the word 'angel'.

The idea that technological and telecommunications systems are an update of the message-bearing angel myth is explored in the film *City of Angels* (1998). The heart surgeon, Dr Maggie Rice (Meg Ryan), asks if her love object, an angel called Seth (Nicolas Cage), is bringing her a message: "I already have... You've definitely been beeped", he says flirtatiously. Rice is left looking perplexed because her hospital pager hasn't gone off. Elsewhere, Seth comforts an air-traffic controller high up in LAX's control tower while watching planes ascending and descending. He later sits on the wing of a stationary Boeing 747 in a hangar, prefiguring the moment when he will become human, and be unable, literally, to take off.

Old-fashioned angels are also being updated to cope with the computer age. The Pope named his trinity of Internet servers at the Vatican after Michael, Gabriel and Raphael, the three most popular archangels in the Catholic church.[2] New Age self-help guides suggest writing special requests on paper and "mailing" them to the angels[3]: for years, angels have put in a frequent appearance on stamps from around the world. New Age guides even advise asking for help from the 'angel of the word-processor'. These days, fabricated 'Technology Angels' battle for supremacy alongside the Archangel Gabriel, the Catholic patron for communications, who has been transformed into the angel of the Internet and laptop.

---

[1] Tobit 12:15-21: "I am Raphael, one of the seven angels who stand ever ready to enter the presence of the glory of the Lord... I am about to return to him above who sent me... And he rose in the air. When they stood up again, he was no longer visible." Michel Serres. *Angels: A modern myth*, tr. Francis Cowper (Paris, Flammarion, 1993), p. 7.

[2] Ruth Gledhill. 'The welcome return of angels to earth', *The Times* (29 November 1998), p. 19.   [3] Taylor. *Messengers of Light*, pp. 70-3.

... LIES INTERRED. THE BODY
OF Mrs ANNE CLERKE. SPINSTER
WHO DIED OCTOBER X. MDCCCXI.
IN THE LXXIII. YEAR OF HER AGE.

IN PEACE WITH GOD, & IN CHARITY.

THE BODY OF Mrs ...
RELICT OF PAUL HENRY MATY.
LATE OF THE BRITISH MUSEUM.
AGED LXXVIII YEARS.
WHO DIED ON THE XXIV. DAY
OF NOVEMBER MDCCCXII.

"An old lady who was in hospital was almost asleep one night when she looked across to another old lady, whom she knew was very ill. At the bottom of the old lady's bed stood an angel not quite on the floor but slightly above. She knew with absolute certainty that the angel had come to take the old lady to heaven."

A woman who believes in the existence of angels

In Memory of
HENRY MORLEY Esq
who died
September 21st 1800
Aged 77
Years.

Dark Angels

Moral ambiguity has been all but eradicated from our present infatuation with divine messengers. Where once it was difficult to deduce whether an individual angel flew for the side of good or evil, modern angels are seen as synonymous with protection and ease. In Ephesians, a wary St Paul advised putting on the "whole armour of God" to guard against both fallen and unfallen angels (Ephesians 6:11-12). Even today, in non-western religions, the distinction between good and evil demons remains less clear-cut than in the West; where the term 'angel' neatly divides the benevolent 'daimon' (the Greek term for supernatural powers) from the malevolent, and heaven from hell.

Fallen angels do not exist in the Old Testament, but an omnipotent God encapsulating the principles both of creation and destruction, employed angels to reward the good and punish the wicked. Angels as manifestations of this shadow side of God could be merciless when executing the divine will. In Ezekiel 9, angels slaughtered old and young, while "evil angels" were sent to strike a plague on the ungrateful Israelites in Psalm 78. As God became more distant and more merciful in later Old Testament times, angels underwent a moral metamorphosis. God was less likely to intervene directly in human affairs and thus the need for spiritual intermediaries, both good and bad, increased. But the emergence of a dualistic religious principle, a good entity versus a separate evil one – the Christian Satan – was a long, convoluted process with eclectic origins.

The Old Testament makes reference only to *ha-satan*, 'the Adversary', which is without diabolic association. But by the second century AD, Satan had become the symbol of evil, an early prototype of the Miltonic archangel who rebelled through pride: "And there was war in heaven: Michael and his angels fought against the dragon; and the dragon fought and his angels," (Revelation 12:7). Christianity, which preaches redemption after a fall of some kind, needed the devil and his fallen angels to provide sins to be overcome, but the myth of Satan – an allegory of man's separation from God – took on a graphically literal form in Christian art. Inspired by passages in Revelation, artists painted good and bad angels battling for the dying man's soul to demonstrate the eternal triumph of good over evil, just as Dr Faustus is advised by rival good and evil angels in Marlowe's Renaissance play.

The concept of hell was largely a medieval invention. With the growth of magic, alchemy and cabbalistic study, it was believed that angels and demons could be summoned for good or diabolic purposes. The medieval mind crystallized all articles of faith into energetic images. The horned devil evolved from lustful Pan, and other threatening pagan gods were re-shaped and cast into hell. Since only angels can have beautiful bird wings, inhabitants of the abyss were invested with wings of bats and reptilian features associative of the dragon, the serpent and creatures of the night. Hieronymus Bosch most famously embodied these fears in his fantastic hybrids of man and beast.

While evil holds a perpetual fascination, hell and the devil as a personification of evil are no longer potent cultural touchstones. A recent doctrinal commission report admitted that the iconography of damnation had been used in the past as a tool of oppression,[1] and stated that hell was probably a place of non-existence: "Hell is not eternal torment, but it is the final and irrevocable choosing of that which is opposed to God so completely and so absolutely that the only end is total non-being." [2] As the idealism of the early twentieth century was crushed by war, genocide and disease, hell turned into other people, as Sartre suggested, or life on earth.

People want their angels to be antidotes to this reality, fantastical intimations of immortality. Contemporary images of devilish angels, as in the film, *God's Army* (also known as *The Prophecy*, Gregory Widen, 1994), in which a priest turned policeman is caught in a Revelation-style battle between good and evil angels, are extremely rare. Dark angels are more likely to be subsumed into antitypes in the superhero genre. In *Darkman* (Sam Raimi, 1990), Liam Neeson plays a synthetic skin scientist who loses his face when his laboratory is blown up and he is left in a vat of caustic chemicals. He turns into an avenging angel who wears a series of masks to hide his disfigurement.

Today, while the evangelistic Christian camp gives credence to angels and balances this with a strong belief in their spiritual opponents, demons, New Agers have managed, by a huge suppressive effort, to banish malevolent spirits entirely from their world view.

[1] "In the past the imagery of hellfire and eternal torment and punishment, often sadistically expressed, has been used to frighten men and women into believing. Christians have professed appalling theologies which made God into a sadistic monster and left searing psychological scars on many." The Doctrine Commission of the Church of England. *The Mystery of Salvation* (1995), p. 199.

[2] Ibid.

Angel of Death

The ancient idea of an angel who plucks the soul from the body at the moment of death has been revived by recent reports of deathbed visions, in which a compassionate angelic figure appears as a guide to the afterlife. The Angel of Death, now evoked as Angel of Everlasting Life, was once portrayed as a beggar, skeleton or reaper, who in Jewish folklore stands between earth and sky wielding a poison-dripping sword.[1]

Historically, the Angel of Death adopted a range of guises. He does not appear in the Bible, and is not to be confused with wrathful Old Testament "destroying angels" or "messengers of death" (Proverbs 16:14). In post-biblical writings, he evolved from non-western death gods into a nightmarish creature, identified in the Talmud with Satan: Satan seduced a female angel called Sin, creating Death from this diabolic union. In folkloric tales he appears as a bloodthirsty anti-hero, or as a stupid figure who can be defeated by human cunning. He may even be moved by compassion to spare young life.

According to a number of witnesses, a similarly benevolent angelic figure may sometimes appear to the dying. Stories of those who have been aware of a 'being of light', or who have called out to an invisible person prior to death, are popular among writers of angel encounter books. These experiences support the notion – reassuring in a society which attempts to sanitize and separate itself from the reality of death – that the 'grim reaper' is more friend than foe. This somewhat contrived view of the angelic is explored in the film *City of Angels* (1998), in which angel Seth leads a little girl wearing pyjamas and clutching a teddy bear along a tunnel of heavenly light. Seth later watches over emergency operations, waiting to escort, rather than extract souls.

The appearance of brilliant light and radiant beings at the point of death may of course be attributed to physical phenomena: encounters with the spirit world have been induced by physical exhaustion, pain and drugs for thousands of years. Journeying through a long, dark tunnel before encountering radiant angels or Christ figures, who act as heralds to the transcendental realms, are also features of modern versions of the shamanistic rite: the near-death and out-of-body experience. These, too, are being reported in growing numbers in North America.

Angels are sometimes perceived in an otherwise inexplicable scent of flowers. Anecdotally at least, it is not uncommon for hospital nurses to notice an unusually strong smell of flowers at the time of a death. This odour, which appears to have no physical explanation, has also been compared to wild garlic. In Michael Powell and Emeric Pressburger's 1946 film, *A Matter of Life and Death*, Conductor 71 is a French angel dispatched to collect David Niven when he bales out of a burning plane. Having failed to escort Niven to heaven at his appointed hour owing to thick fog which obscures the plane, the angel meets with him on earth. Amusingly, Niven's character associates his angel of death with the smell of fried onions, although he has first appeared to him among fragrant rose bushes.

Writings by Muslim visionaries express ambivalence toward the deathly apparition. One theory is that Azrael, the Islamic Angel of Death, may appear in a form commensurate with the life lived. Thus one man can die of a scent of roses, and another of a foul smell. Another notion is that the soul actually falls in love with Azrael, and is seduced from its body. Great prophets like Moses were even gently invited by death who took corporeal form. In mythic terms, Love and Death, Eros and Thanatos are paralleled. Love may be represented as a starving, shrivelled creature, while death can appear as a handsome young man.[2]

[1] Peter Lamborn Wilson *Angels: Messengers of the gods* (London, Thames and Hudson, 1994), p. 55. [2] Ibid.

Graveyards

Stone-carved angels, particularly the sympathetic, feminine variety, cluster around Victorian tombstones and crosses. With their protective wings, simple tunics and bare feet, they stand on tiptoe with arms outstretched to heaven, or look piously toward flowers clasped as symbols of immortality. Others perch on imposing beds of stone high in the air, or recline on the grass in languorous poses more indicative of ennui than of concern for their dead charges. Today, some have had their wings clipped by weather, or are suspended at precarious angles grafted onto subsiding crosses. Some have grown accidental haloes made from briars and birds' nests. A few have been unceremoniously kicked to the ground.

From the thirteenth century, angels played an integral role among the effigies in celestial tomb tableaux, which were designed to show the paradisiacal life that awaited the blessed. Above the processions of saints, they were shown carrying the soul of the recumbent figure to the feet of Christ in heaven. Alternatively, the angels were depicted adoring Christ, while the soul in the guise of a man, managed its independent migration. On less elaborate tombs, angels or cherubs held aloft plaques inscribed with epitaphs or heraldic shields. Winged, childlike heads popularized during the Renaissance, continued to decorate English headstones until the early nineteenth century.

A striking motif that appeared in Italy in the seventeenth century was the winged skeleton. It was portrayed emerging from an open tomb carrying a sculpted or painted portrait of the deceased. By carrying the soul to heaven or purgatory, it performed one of the roles of the guardian angel. The flying skeleton or winged skull looks like a sinister hybrid, a cross between angel and devil, yet it represented the travails of earthly life in an age in which life was perceived as being close to death. It also prefigured the moment of resurrection when the soul would be reunited with and would reanimate the body.[1] In the eighteenth century angels frequently appeared on funerary monuments, showing increasing concern for the dead. In one Italian tomb sculpture, an angel presides over the disordered bones in a charnel box, contemplating whether to rearrange them into skeletal shape.[2]

The Victorians sculpted religious icons in an attempt to preserve the solidity of a Christian universe which was being eroded by science and the industrial revolution. The evangelicals looked back to the medieval era – the height of angelicism – as an age of faith. Angels re-emerged, not as living creatures but as graveside guardians who mimicked the exaggerated passions of grieving relatives, thus reflecting this doomed search for spiritual revival.

Victorian families obsessively built grief and remembrance into their daily lives. They made frequent pilgrimages to cemeteries, and the wealthy erected theatrical statues incorporating living and deceased figures which maintained family unity in spite of the rupture of death. The deaths of children were considered the most unacceptable: although medical advances and humanitarian concern had increased life expectancy, in 1840 one in four children in lower class families still died before the age of five. Angels had been associated with women and children since the fifteenth century, but female angels now became children's symbolic companions on tombstones and in paintings.

Parents immortalized their offspring in life-size statues and postures designed to arouse maximum pathos. Angels superseded the weeping mother as heavenly guardian, and symbolizing innocence and beauty, exalted the 'angelic' virtues of the child. Angels leaned over effigies of bewildered children, preparing to lift them heavenward, and cherubs drew embroidered cloths over stone babies dying in petrified cribs. Children's tombs, which only became clearly defined in the late eighteenth century, had overrun the cemeteries by the 1850s.

[1] Philipe Ariès. *Images of Man and Death,* tr. Janet Lloyd (Harvard University Press, 1985), p. 187-8.
[2] Church of the Santi Apostoli, Rome. Ibid., p. 187.

"I brought my Tamagochi to school but I couldn't feed it so it died. It came as an angel up to heaven."

Five-year-old boy

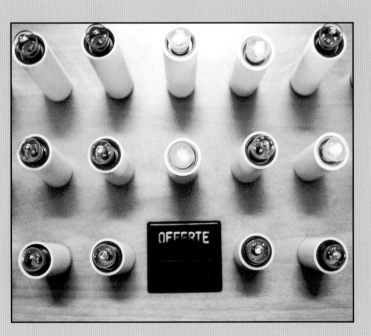

Eroticism

Contact with the angelic realm was perceived by some ancient societies as involving a heightened, though non-diabolic erotic state: the shaman, for example, is meant to 'marry' his guardian spirit.[1] Angels are presumed to be bodiless, genderless and hence genetically chaste, yet in certain traditions, have always been sexually ambiguous.

In early rabbinic and occult lore a few female angels appeared alongside their male counterparts. Most were benevolent; a minority were lascivious and disobedient. The Christian church repressed the Judaic tradition which tells how the notorious angel, Lilith, was created as Adam's first wife. Rebelling against the patriarchal hegemony which insisted she put up with the missionary position, Lilith flew off to beget a hundred offspring a day from more adventurous demons. In hell, she became Satan's favourite bride, one of the angels of prostitution. Night-time visits by her daughters, the Lilim or succubi, were blamed for the wet dreams of celibate monks, who tried to protect themselves by tying crucifixes to their genitals.[2]

Male angels were also vulnerable to sins of the flesh. St Paul's cryptic remark that women ought to wear veils "because of the angels" (1 Corinthians 11:10), refers back to Genesis, which briefly mentions that, in the days before Noah, concupiscent angels came to earth and took "daughters of men" as their wives (Genesis 6:2-4). These mortal women gave birth to gigantic offspring called Nephilim. Although the Israelites were afraid to enter an "evil" land filled with these superbeings (Numbers 13:32-3), the Nephilim are also described in glowing terms as "mighty men which were of old, men of renown" (Genesis 6:4).

The early Christian church, which considered the angels of God to be pure and incorruptible, adopted the apocryphal Book of Enoch's interpretation of the incident as the origin of evil. According to Enoch, two hundred angels of fire who were supposed to be assisting the archangels in the creation of Eden, descended to earth against God's will. The fallen angels were transformed into flesh before defiling mortal women. Their 11,250 feet tall offspring were cannibalistic warmongers who were eventually murdered by loyal angels, while their fathers were tossed into hell.

The humanistic poet, John Milton, seems to have been unaware of these esoteric traditions. However, in *Paradise Lost*, he dispensed with the Aquinan view of angels as pure spirits, and re-interpreted the angels, both fallen and unfallen, as being able to make love solely for sexual pleasure. They can also switch between genders or opt for a form of hermaphroditism at will: "those male, / These feminine. For spirits when they please / Can either sex assume, or both; so soft / And uncompounded is their essence pure," (I 423-31). William Blake celebrated Milton's libidinous, very human angels, who reveal the divine possibilities of human sexuality. Blake believed that humanity could not progress without the creative opposition of body and soul, imagination and reason, which had been split by conventional religion. He expounded this philosophy in *The Marriage of Heaven and Hell*, in which he inverted the usual principles so that good becomes evil and heaven is hell. Blake's Satan is transformed into the personification of energy and goodness, and he satirized Swedenborg's angels, who stand for rationality and wickedness.

Wings of Desire (1987), and its American adaptation, *City of Angels* (1998), use angelic anthropomorphism to show the significance of human love: angels in both films can only fall in love with humans. In *Wings of Desire*, Damiel is fascinated by a circus trapeze artist who wears an angel's costume, while in *City of Angels*, Seth falls in love with a heart surgeon. The angels must become mortal in order to experience the fullness of love, which includes sensuous and sensual pleasure.

The recent trend in the West has been to divest angelic sexuality of its erotic power, just as the lustful Greek god Eros was once translated into the more romantically inclined Cupid. The angelic hero of Nora Ephron's film, *Michael* (1996), engages in a schmaltzy version of the seductive, or seducible, angel myth: John Travolta as Archangel Michael oozes an aphrodisiac chocolate-smelling body odour, which proves irresistible to women. Elsewhere, angelic eroticism has been displaced from the heavens and downgraded into a pseudo-sexual fantasy. Today, Sharon Stone is photographed wearing a white bikini top, trousers and wings; and the model, Tyra Banks, parades lingerie wearing up-tilting, phallic wings on the catwalk.

[1] Wilson. *Angels*, p. 65.
[2] Godwin. *Angels*, p. 89.

Ghosts

Since most authorities insist that angels were conceived as a separate order of creation, it is impossible for humans to be transformed into angels after death. In the whole history of angelology, there have been just a handful of extraordinary exceptions. Enoch, the father of Methuselah, was apotheosized into the great angel, Metatron, sometimes called 'the lesser Yahweh': "And Enoch walked with God: and he was not; for God took him" (Genesis 5:24). Jacob became Israel, who is identified with the angel Uriel, while Elijah was translated into the angel Sandalphon. There is an esoteric tradition that insists St Francis evolved into the angel Rhamiel.

In spite of this lack of precedent, it is not uncommon to find confusion between angels and ghosts. There is a widespread contemporary belief that, after death, relatives and close friends can be transformed into benevolent angelic beings who hover protectively around the bereaved. In a recent poll, 15% of North Americans identified angels as spirits of the dead.[1] And in 1987, a survey of British religious experience found that 35% of people who had an awareness of the presence of someone who had died, interpreted this as religious.[2] Contemporary accounts of angelic visitations often feature dead people as winged figures, surrounded by bright light and floating above the ground. The dead person may, however, be borne aloft by angelic guardians. Others believe that deceased relatives serve as their guardian angels.

Envisaging angels as Manes, or the semi-deified souls of departed spirits, shows the collapsing of the distance between human and divine in the western imagination. The notion may have been adopted from non-western cultures which hold that human souls evolve eventually into protecting angels. Benevolent spirits called *shen* in Chinese religion are often thought to be the ghosts of ancestors. *Shen* can be called upon to serve the living through ritual and sacrifice. In Shinto, *kami* are spirits of deities, ancestors and natural objects, who can be enlisted by prayer and devotion. Certain western traditions support similar beliefs. The Swedish mining engineer and mystic, Emanuel Swedenborg (1688-1772), believed that the souls of dead people may become angels sometimes to assist humans with their spiritual development. Nineteenth-century commemorative pictures depicting angelic apparitions hovering over graveside mourners, suggest that the Victorians believed their dead relatives might communicate as angels.

Today, referring to dead people as angels seems to be a fashionable way of explaining feelings of proximity to deceased loved ones, and of preserving an emotional connection. The term 'angel' is preferable in the current climate to the morally ambivalent 'ghost'. The trend may be a form of sentimental wish fulfilment, encouraged by films like *A Matter of Life and Death* (1946), which dole out wings to the recently deceased: on arrival in heaven, each dead fighter pilot receives a pair of pristine wings encased in a transparent plastic bag. In *What Dreams May Come* (Vincent Ward, 1998), the dead Dr Chris Nielsen (Robin Williams) is able to fly around heaven even without the aid of wings.

Since many people imagine that heaven is populated with angels and dead humans, they may be comforted by the idea that their loved ones are cohabiting with the angels. It is perhaps even more appealing to imagine that they are transformed after death into celestial beings.

[1] *Time*, December 1995. A further 55% defined angels as "higher spiritual beings created by God with special powers to act as his agents on earth."

[2] Michael Argyle. 'The psychological perspective on religious experience', 2nd Series Occasional Paper 8 (Oxford, Religious Experience Research Centre, Westminster College, 1997), p. 6-7.

Aliens

Some people believe that the wheeled beings which Ezekiel, Elijah and Enoch saw in fantastic visions were not, in fact, angels, but ancient space travellers. Ezekiel says: "And when the living creatures went, the wheels went by them: and when the living creatures were lifted up from the earth, the wheels were lifted up" (Ezekiel 1:19). The creatures, which each have four faces and four wings, rose out of a whirlwind, clouds and fire, and moved forward synchronously on fiery wheels without turning to the sides. It was from this vision which took place around 560 BC that medieval scholars derived the third order of angels known as wheels or thrones.

In the 1950s, when UFOs were being popularized, Jung described flying saucers as an emerging modern myth, the bearers of technological and salvationist fantasies. He called them technological angels, angelic images for an age he thought incapable of believing in the supernatural. Owing to their mysterious origins, and the collective strength of the desire to believe in them, UFOs have been invested with quasi-religious significance since the first attempts at recording proof on photographic plates. Many symbols of alleged religious supernatural events have reappeared in UFO sightings. They emerge from the sky, regarded as the sacred sphere in Judaeo-Christian and Islamic cultures, and propel themselves aerially on seemingly weightless discs, wheels or saucers, appearing to levitate by neutralizing the earth's gravity. Some witnesses insist that UFOs and their alien inhabitants have healing powers, which have cured them of serious medical complaints.

There are further connections between angels and aliens. According to accounts, both can have shining eyes and an other-worldly glow. Witnesses suggest that UFOs have come to guide humanity; they thus appear to perform the key, defining role of message-bearing angels. Sightings and science fiction contain frequent references to the notion of morally, spiritually or technologically superior alien beings bringing warnings to mankind. Extraterrestrials seem to offer more global directives, while angels communicate individual messages, but both address themselves to specific witnesses. Like angels, aliens also seem to be accomplished linguists, able to communicate with witnesses in their own language.[1] Two per cent of Americans claim to have been abducted by aliens (comparable to the notion of angels who come to earth to fetch souls), which is a more recent aspect of the UFO myth. In more sinister stories, which involve aliens subjecting humans to nightmarish operations, extraterrestrials perform a role akin to that of the fallen angels.

Some take parallels between the two types of airborne being further, arguing that aliens are actual angels, or that angels are alien frauds. Christian evangelicals have speculated that UFOs could be part of God's angelic host who preside over universal creation, while fundamendalists have suggested the opposite, that increased UFO sightings imply an intensification of satanic activity. Members of the cult, Heaven's Gate, which preached a strange mixture of Christianity and alien-abduction lore, committed mass suicide in 1997 believing they were about to join a spaceship travelling to heaven in the wake of the comet Hale-Bopp. Some millenarians are even convinced that the heavens are riven with both benevolent and malevolent UFO-angels, gearing up to wage an apocalyptic war between good and evil.

Symbolizing otherness, UFOs, like angels, have become the focus for our dreams, erotic fantasies and fears. Since they incorporate the angelic characteristic of flight and are believed to guide humanity, UFOs appear to be a technological updating of the potent angel archetype, a psychic symbol that has reappeared in a new guise with the decline of organized religion. As the UFO phenomenon grows, angels are simultaneously being re-invented as pseudo or semi-religious cult figures.

It is a sign of the times that we have not only revisited the supernatural as a repository for displaced spirtual concerns, but have begun to conflate the technological with the supernatural, the UFO with the angel. Belief in UFOs, like belief in modern angels, seems to offer the hope of redemption, and fear of damnation, outside standard religious structures.

---

[1] Gustav Davidson suggests that Hebrew is probably the lingua franca of angels, and of all other spirits, in *A Dictionary of Angels*, p. xix.

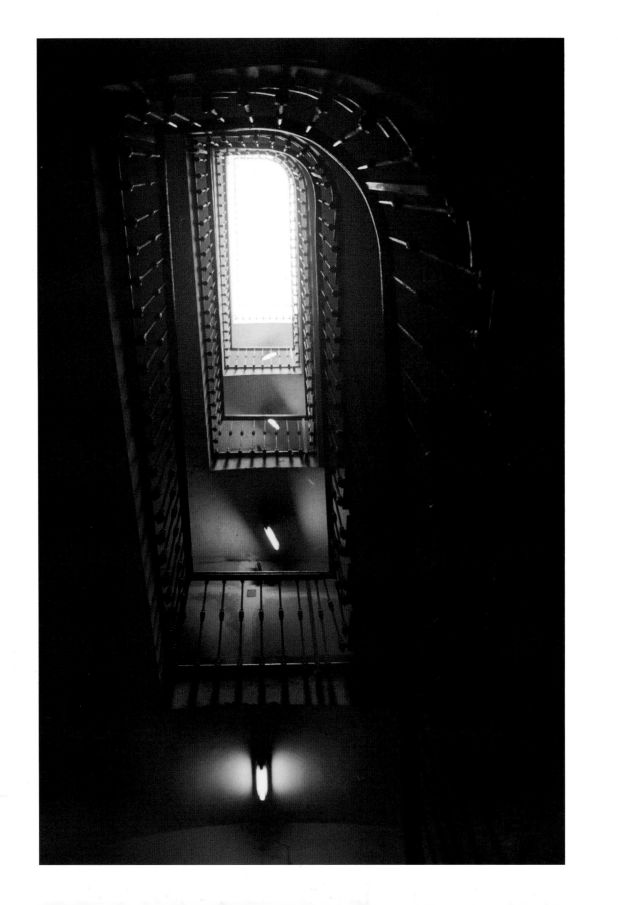

ACKNOWLEDGEMENTS

Seraphim are deeply grateful to the following actors, friends and acquaintances who have modelled for photographs: Zara Balfour, Elizabeth Barrett, Peter Bailey, Ruth Brennon, Jason Cooper, Vicky Copestake, Fenella D'Addio, Hillary Day, Paul Delves, Carmel and Maria Doohan, Kate Gabriel, Catherine Gill, Ellie and Kate Healey, Anthony Houghton, Angela Kaye, Darren McGavin, Charlotte and Natasha McKeever, Masayo Matsushita, Carmel Morrissey, Kate Millner, Rowenna Mortimer, Liza Nicklin, Elayne O'Neale, Joanna Rudge, Katy Slater, Louise Taylor, Myron Thompson Junior, Myron Thompson Senior, Keiran Walker, Sarah White, Holly Wilkinson, Elaine Wilson.

Seraphim are deeply grateful for the assistance and support they have received from the following individuals and organizations: Joe Ahearne; Arts & Business Placement Scheme: Sarah Davies, Jenni Francis and Linda Griffiths; Julian and Mary Ashby; Jan Bek; Brian Benton; Birmingham Museum & Art Gallery: Brendan Flynn (Curator of Paintings) and Dave Lucas; Adrian D. Bland, Chair, Ikon Gallery Board; Maggie Brace; the British Red Cross Society; Ceri and Saul Burness; Bridget Burt; Olga Boada; CBC Ltd: George Fleming, Andy Madgwick, George Makin and Phil Millership; Ned and Sage Conran; Cristina Contessi; Sabrina Del Pret; Robert Dowland; Glennyce Eckersley; Nicola Edmonds at Vivid; Ely Cathedral: Verger Matthew Austin and Heather Kilpatrick; Endsleigh Builders Ltd; Derek Frampton; Dr Steve Hajioff; Halladay's Drop Forgings Ltd; Patricia and Robin Hart; Emma Heathcote; Christine Homer; David Hutchison at the Electric Cinema; International Alliance of Guardian Angels: Richard Hoseason (UK Co-ordinator) and David King of the London chapter; Donya James; Esther Jeapes; Steve Jones at Palm Laboratory; Richard Julian; Rafal Kaniewski; Reg Keiling; Jonathan Knight at St Paul's Church Project, Islington; David Laird; Sue Lawson; Leon Lazaveric; Naomi Leake; Helene Marshallsay; Jasmine McKeever; Mungo Maclaghan; Bobby Mayley; Chris and Patricia Mitford; Sally Morfil; Sam Nicol and the children at Dallington School; Anthony and David O'Leary; Osbourne Office: Denise Bull, Liz Gately, Sarah Perry, Kirsty Organ and Geraldine Whiteshaw; Jacqueline Perkins; Neil Phillips at E. S. Phillips Studios, Lightwoods Park; Quatro Paper Ltd; Sue Ribbans; Diane Robertson at Madame Tussauds; Deborah Robinson at Walsall Museum & Art Gallery; St Chad's Cathedral, Birmingham: Father Patrick Daley, Father John Sharpe and Sheila Williams; St Nicholas RC Junior School, Sutton Coldfield; Emma Shiel; Varinder Sunsoa; Mike Terry; Town School, Sutton Coldfield; Kevin Treadwell; G. Treglown Associates Ltd; Antonio Trimani; Helen Turner and St Martin's Parish Church, Birmingham; Brenda Ward; West Midlands Arts: Jenny Hayes, Deborah Klomp and Martin Turner; Kevin Waugh; Rev Tom Willis; Rhonda Wilson at Seeing the Light; Keith Woodley; Julie Wright.

Carl Burness would particularly like to thank Graham Treglown and Mark Burness, without whose generous assistance it would not have been possible to print this book. Justina Hart would especially like to thank Rev David Lomax, who has provided invaluable moral and practical support, including informal tutorials at The Swedenborg Society, Bloomsbury; generous loan of materials and detailed comments on the text.